DIARY
OF A
MIDDLE SCHOOL
ZOMBIE

No Zombie Left Behind

ZACK ZOMBIE

JUNE

Nice To Meet You

Hi.

I'm a zombie.

AND THIS IS MY DIARY.

I know. You've probably never heard of a zombie that had a diary.

You've probably never even heard of a zombie that could read and write.

But that's me. I'm a zombie. I can read and write, and I have a diary.

I kind of wish it was a journal, though. Sounds a little more **MANLY**.

But when you're a zombie, you've got to take whatever you can get.

Embarrassing, I know.

Now, if you're reading this diary, that probably means either I'm dead or you have a really weird preoccupation with zombies.

Since I'm still. . .err. . .alive, you might want to talk to somebody about your **ZOMBIE FETISH**.

It's okay.

I won't judge.

I think I'm twelve years old.

Or at least that's how old they said I was when I died.

I can't remember anything about my life before I was a zombie.

Not many zombies can.

Last thing I remember was coming out of the ground and **HAVING BUGS IN MY TEETH.**

I had bugs in other parts too, but I'm too embarrassed to talk about that right now.

At least my situation was better than some other zombies I know.

One zombie came out missing a leg.

Another zombie came out **MISSING BOTH OF HIS ARMS.**

One zombie even came out without a head.

Yeah, he had a real hard time getting around.

Or it could've been a "she."

Nobody could tell.

Now, the **GOOD THING** about being a zombie is that we don't grow old.

Like, I've been twelve years old for about five years now.

It's kind of cool being a young zombie, though.

Except when I want to get into R-rated movies.

The people at the movie theater don't believe me when I tell them how old I really am.

I think maybe it's because of my **DIMPLES**.

I guess having holes in your face means that you're really young around here.

Where Do Zombies Come From?

Now you're probably wondering how I became a zombie.

For a long time I had a hard time figuring it out, too.

I asked a lot of other zombies, but they didn't know either.

Yeah, I know. Zombies aren't really that **SMART**.

I finally got answers from my social worker, Kenya.

Kenya said that zombies came because of **GLOBAL WARMING**.

It kind of makes sense . . .

I heard global warming causes everything.

So I decided to do some **RESEARCH ON ZOMBIES**.

But where I live, they don't let us use the internet.

They get really mad if you do.

Luckily, Kenya lets me use her computer sometimes. She's really nice like that.

I started watching YouTube videos that talked about where zombies came from.

I like **YOUTUBE VIDEOS**. They're really funny.

Especially the ones that show humans running into things.

I swear they look just like zombies.

I found a bunch of videos that explained where zombies came from.

One video said zombies came from a **MILITARY EXPERIMENT** that went wrong.

Another video said that zombies came after somebody ate a fifty-year-old Twinkie.

There was even a video that said zombies came after somebody accidentally spilled some **LIME SODA**.

Yeah . . . Didn't make sense to me either.

But there was one video that made a lot more sense.

It said that because of global warming, some large frozen islands in the Arctic Ocean melted . . .

Then the ice released some ancient mold spores that floated in the air. . .

Eventually, the spores got sucked into the clouds and created rain that landed on a lot of **GRAVEYARDS** . . .

And next thing you know, **DEAD PEOPLE** started popping out of their graves and walking into towns looking for brains.

BRAINS.

Gross, I know.

The Zombie Apocalypse

That video also said that when the first zombies came out, it started something called the **ZOMBIE APOCALYPSE**.

It's kind of a weird name.

Especially since zombies don't have lips.

Anyway, the humans really didn't know what to do. So they just ran for their lives.

They did everything they could to hide from getting their brains eaten by zombies.

Then one day, somebody got the idea to hide out in a McDonald's restaurant.

I guess they thought that the McDonald's smell would repel the zombies.

But it actually had the opposite effect.

For some reason, the zombies were attracted to McDonald's restaurants.

Everywhere there was a McDonalds, you could find a zombie.

That's why you can find zombies on every continent now.

Over 100 Million Served. . .

Then somebody had the crazy idea of giving a zombie a McDonald's **CHICKEN NUGGET**.

I guess the guy must have been desperate.

Well, the video said that after the zombie ate the chicken nugget, something strange happened.

Some people say that it was the "special" secret ingredients in the chicken nugget . . .

Or the festive McDonald's atmosphere. . .

But, all of a sudden, the zombie didn't want brains anymore.

Just more **NUGGETS!**

Next thing you know, zombies everywhere were crazy about nuggets.

Instead of brains, they just wanted nuggets. And they would do anything for them.

Eventually, the zombies left the humans alone, and they flocked to every McDonald's restaurant they could find looking for nuggets.

Now, the humans realized that they could **CONTROL** the zombies.

So humans started giving the zombies as many chicken nuggets as they wanted.

Then, everything **CALMED DOWN**.

So thanks to a chicken nugget, it put an end to the Zombie Apocalypse and saved the human world.

Too Many Zombies

Soon, the humans realized that there were way too many zombies.

So they had to figure out how to **GET RID OF** all the zombies.

Somebody suggested to just throw them in the ocean.

But zombies don't need to breathe, so that didn't work.

Then somebody came up with the idea of using fire to get rid of them.

But instead of burning, the zombies just got a **NICE TAN**. . .and a strong, lingering smell of bacon.

Then they tried to use **ACID** to get rid of the zombies.

But the acid just made the zombies giggle uncontrollably.

Then somebody came up with the idea of **SHOOTING** zombies into outer space.

They thought that zombies couldn't cause any trouble out there.

But for some reason, the zombies just kept getting sucked back into earth's orbit.

And next thing you know, there were **ZOMBIE METEORS** raining down on unsuspecting towns all across America.

Zombie Village

Eventually, they decided to just take all zombies and put them in Villages.

Kind of like **SUMMER CAMP** for zombies, except it's year-round.

And that's where I live today.

It's not so bad here.

Actually, I kind of like it.

But the electric fence really smarts sometimes.

Now, I wish they would let us do things like watch TV, play video games or use a cell phone.

But there is a strict **"NO SCREENS"** rule in the village.

27

I guess they think that TV and video games will rot our brains.

Yeah, humans can be kind of weird sometimes.

Like, what's wrong with a rotten brain anyway?

SCREEN WILL ROT YOUR BRAIN

Now, Kenya did let me use her **CELL PHONE** once.

But I accidentally swallowed it.

Actually, it wasn't an accident . . . I just didn't want to get caught.

But the cool thing was that Kenya wasn't really mad.

She just wanted her phone back.

It took about a week, but I finally got it back.

And it worked great!

Eventually the **BURNT CHEESE AND GARLIC SMELL** went away too. . .

Well . . . sort of.

My Cool Name

Hey! I never told you my name.

My name is Zombie, but you can call me "Z."

Actually, my real name is **Z06578**.

At least that's what the people at the zombie village call me.

I think it's because that's the number on my membership card.

ZOMBIE RECORD
NAME - UNKNOWN
NUMBER - Z06578
HEIGHT - 4' 11"
EYES YES NO
HAIR COLOR - BLACK

We all get cool names like that.

Like my bunkmate's name is ZO7734.

When you look at his name upside down it looks like it says, **"HELLO Z."**

So I just call him Z.

The only problem is, I think everybody got the same idea.

Now when somebody yells "Z!" across the village, like a **THOUSAND ZOMBIES** turn their heads.

And because most zombie's heads aren't screwed on very tight, they fall off really easy.

So when somebody yells "Z!" it sounds like it's raining watermelons.

No Zombie Left Behind

Everything started changing around here a few years ago, right after the **NEW PRESIDENT** was elected.

The new president decided since zombies used to be people, then under the constitution they should have rights too.

So she passed a law that gave zombies the same rights as regular people.

So the zombies in all the villages across the country had to be **RELOCATED**.

Now, they didn't really know what to do with all the zombie kids like me.

So they decided to put us up for **ADOPTION**.

They called it the "No Zombie Left Behind" campaign.

That started about two years ago.

But in the past two years, there hasn't ever been one zombie kid who's been adopted.

I don't really understand why.

I think zombies make good **PETS**.

My Zombie Friends

One of my good friends at my zombie village is a zombie called **OLD MAN JENKINS**.

Old Man Jenkins was one of the first zombies ever.

He said he's been around since the Zombie Apocalypse.

He even said he was one of the first zombies to ever taste chicken nuggets.

He said they were finger-licking good.

It wouldn't be so bad, except he ended up eating a few of those, too.

Whenever I need some advice, I always go to Old Man Jenkins.

That's because he's really smart about things of the world.

Like, I think that maybe before he was a zombie, he must've been a **PROFESSOR OR A SCIENTIST**.

Or a reality show host or something.

I also have a few other good friends that are zombies.

Their names are **NED, ZED,** and **FRED.**

Since they're triplets, we're all always trying to figure out how they all became zombies at the same time.

The leading theory is that they were clones, and they were part of the same military experiment.

It would explain why they keep finishing each other's sentences.

And why they're joined at the hip.

My First Human Friend

My favorite hobby is watching YouTube videos.

Sometimes, Kenya lets me use her laptop to watch them.

But it's not allowed here, so I only get to do it once in a while.

Kenya said that I'm **ADDICTED** to watching YouTube videos.

I think she doesn't really like me watching them.

She said that they're affecting the way I talk.

But I really don't know what my bae is talkin' about.

FO' SHIZZLE.

Kenya also said that I learn really fast.

She said she thinks I have a photographic memory.

That kind of makes sense.

There's a lot of space up there since I don't have much of a brain.

CAMERA   BRAIN

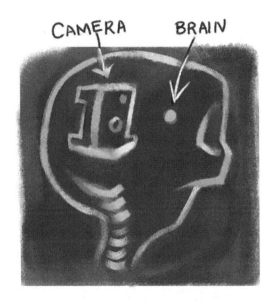

Kenya also taught me how to **READ AND WRITE**.

And I loved writing so much, that she brought me my first diary so I could write my thoughts in it.

Kenya is really nice . . . for a human.

Actually, she's my only human friend.

She said that I remind her of her little brother who died a long time ago.

He was twelve years old like me.

She said that he died of a disease called cancer.

And she always cries when she talks to me about him.

Her little brother's name was **ZACK**.

I like the name Zack.

I wish somebody would give me a cool name like that.

I'm Getting Adopted Today!

I heard that a family was coming to our zombie village to adopt a zombie today.

All the zombie kids were so excited, they didn't know what to do with themselves.

Some kids even tried to **COMB THEIR HAIR** to look better.

But I don't think that was a very good idea.

After they finished, there was like, all this nose hair everywhere.

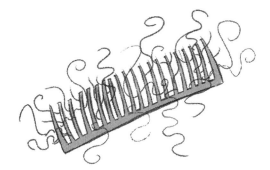

Some zombie kids even tried to brush their teeth.

But I don't think that was a good idea either.

Especially since some kid got his hands on an **ELECTRIC TOOTHBRUSH**.

To this day, I can still find teeth stuck in the walls . . .

. . . and the ceiling.

But you know, I don't really mind.

Because nothing can make me sad today.

I'm going to **DAZZLE** this family so much that they're going to be desperate to take me home.

Wow, I can't believe it.

I might have my own human family.

Man, I can't wait!

Guess Not

Well, so much for getting adopted.

The family that came to visit **CHANGED THEIR MINDS**—really fast.

Somebody said the family was freaked out by all the cameras outside.

Somebody else said that they were scared of getting **ZOMBIE COOTIES**.

But something tells me it might've something else.

Like, I heard the first kid they spoke to still had the electric toothbrush in his hand.

So, not only are there teeth, but there's hair, skin and makeup stuck on the ceiling now.

Man, I should probably give up on any **HOPE** of ever getting adopted.

I mean, who's going to want to adopt a zombie kid anyway?

Good News and Bad News

Today, Kenya came up to my room to see how I was doing.

"Hey, Zombie, how are you feeling?"

"**KIND OF SAD,**" I said. "I was really hoping to get adopted by that family yesterday."

"Yeah, a lot of the other kids were sad too. But you probably wouldn't want to get adopted by that family," Kenya said.

"Why not?"

"They were a bunch of **CLOWNS**."

"Whoa, Kenya, that's not nice!"

"No, really. They were a bunch of clowns. They were here looking for a zombie to join their **CIRCUS ACT**. Something about shooting a zombie out of a cannon or something."

Whoa.

Well, that would explain the makeup on the ceiling.

"So Zombie, I have some good news and some bad news for you," Kenya said. "Which one do you want to hear first?"

"The bad news, I guess," I said, thinking that things couldn't get any worse.

"Well, the bad news is that today is my **LAST DAY** as your social worker," she said with tears in her eyes. "I'm going to be moving to a new facility closer to where I live."

Wow. I couldn't believe what I was hearing.

"Really? But that's **NOT FAIR**," I said. And if I had tears, they would probably be in my eyes too.

"Don't worry, Zombie. You'll find a family. Probably a lot sooner than you think."

Man, yesterday and today have been like, the **WORST DAYS** of my life!

So I just sat there with **MY HEAD HANGING LOW**.

Kenya got a little worried, so she helped pull my head back on my shoulders.

"So, do you want to hear the good news?" Kenya asked me.

"Whatever," I said, depressed. But I could tell Kenya was eager to share it.

"Sigh. . . What is it?"

"How would you like to come with me?"

"WAIT. . .WHAT?"

"I spoke to my supervisors, and they said that I could take you with me."

"Seriously?"

"Yes. And you wouldn't have to stay in a zombie village anymore. You could stay with me and Kyle, my husband. And we'll be your **FOSTER FAMILY**."

Now, I really thought I was hearing things.

"Are you for real?!!!"

"Yes, I'm for real. And it's all been taken care of. All you have to do is say yes and we can leave **TOMORROW**."

Wow. I couldn't believe it.

I was so shocked I started making zombie noises.

"Uuuurrrgggghhh."

Kenya was just sitting there, a little weirded out. But she was still waiting for an answer.

"Well?"

"Yes! **DEFINITELY!** Yeah! **ABSOLUTELY!** Of course!" I said.

"Great! So pack your things and get ready. We can leave tomorrow morning."

That night I couldn't sleep.

I just kept thinking about what my new life would be like.

Whoa. I was finally leaving the zombie village.

And I was going to live with my **FIRST HUMAN FAMILY**!

How amazing is that?

I can imagine it now. . .

But then I started getting a little nervous.

Oh man, I don't even know what humans are like, I thought.

What if they don't like me?

And, I've heard some crazy things about humans.

Like. . .what if they try to **HOMESCHOOL** me?!!!

But, you know, now that I think about it, maybe humans are all really nice, like Kenya.

And maybe being homeschooled is really not that bad. . .

Wow, if that's true, then this whole foster family thing is going to be a **PIECE OF CAKE**!

Okay then. I guess I'm ready.

Look out human world . . .

. . . 'Cause here I come!

Welcome to HumanTown

Well, we finally made it to Kenya's hometown today.

And when we got there, there was a **HUGE SIGN** welcoming us into town.

Whoa. I guess I'm going to be the first zombie in town.

I wonder if they're going to throw me a parade?

I heard on the internet that's what people do when they're glad to see you.

SO AWESOME.

The town looked pretty cool.

There were these tall things all around that Kenya called TREES.

She also said that people lived in these giant boxes called HOUSES.

They also had this green stuff in front of each house that Kenya called GRASS.

And they even had some sweaty guys out front of each HOUSE playing with the green stuff.

I think she called them GARDENERS.

When we got to Kenya's house, I was hoping she would have her own sweaty guy out front.

But her house didn't come with one.

SO SAD.

But she did have a guy fixing some pipes outside her house.

I think she called him a PLUM-BER.

He looked like he could really use a **QUARTER**.

So, I gave him one.

Then, for some reason he ran away, like really fast.

Kenya's house was **BLUE AND WHITE** and had a bunch of windows.

As we walked up to Kenya's house, people around the neighborhood started looking at us with their mouths open.

Then they started pointing at us.

It was kind of a strange way to say hi if you ask me.

But I didn't want to be rude.

So I just said hi back.

It was hard keeping my mouth open, though.

Especially because of all the **BUGS** that kept flying in there.

My New Human Family

When we walked closer to Kenya's house, the front door opened, and a guy came out.

"Zombie, I want you to meet Kyle, my husband," Kenya said.

I looked up and there was a guy standing there with a **CONFUSED** look on his face.

"Hi, Zombie, my name is Kyle," he said.

"Hi, Kyle, I'm Zombie. But you can call me Z," I said.

"Hey, Z," Kyle said, scratching his head.

Later I found out that Kenya had decided to bring me home without telling Kyle.

She said she had just told Kyle about it this morning.

Old Man Jenkins said that meant that Kenya **WORE THE PANTS** in the family.

That kind of made sense. . .

I've only seen Kyle wear JORTS most of the time.

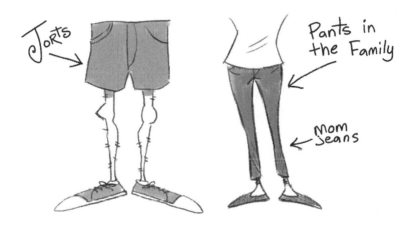

Jorts

Pants in the Family

Mom Jeans

Then I walked into Kenya and Kyle's house.

It was amazing.

They had all these **STRANGELY SHAPED** things all around the house.

I think Kenya called it FUR-NI-TURE.

She told me that since this wasn't the zombie village, I had to treat everything nicely.

I guess she didn't really appreciate me **MARKING MY TERRITORY**.

Suddenly, the front door opened again, and a girl came in, talking on a cell phone.

"Cassie, can you please put your phone away?" Kenya said. "I want to introduce you to someone."

But the girl just kept talking on the phone and didn't really notice we were there.

"Cassie," Kenya said, taking the girl's phone and putting it on the table. "**THIS IS IMPORTANT.**"

Then the girl started making noises and rolling her eyes.

Whoa. And I thought only zombies could do that.

"What's that smell?" the girl said. "It smells like bacon and butt cream."

"Cassie, I want you to meet Zombie. Zombie, this is my daughter Cassie. She's thirteen years old," Kenya said.

The girl just stood there looking at me.

"Hi, Cassie. My name is Zombie. But you can call me Z," I said.

Cassie just rolled her eyes again and took her phone back.

"Don't mind her, Zombie. She's just going through **PUBERTY**," Kenya said.

Yeah, that kind of made sense.

I heard puberty was like deadly for human kids.

"Anyway, Cassie, Zombie is going to be spending some time with us," Kenya said. "So please be nice to him."

I think that was enough to get Cassie off the phone.

"What do you mean he's going to **SPEND TIME WITH US**?"

"He's going to be our special guest for a while," Kenya said.

Then Cassie started making noises and rolling her eyes again.

"Urgh! I hope you didn't give him my room. I am going to have a total **COW** if you did!" she said.

Whoa.

Puberty sounds really painful.

"No, we didn't give him your room. Zombie is going to stay in the attic, for now," Kenya said. "But be nice to him, okay?"

Then Cassie just ran up the stairs and **SLAMMED** the door to her room.

"Don't worry about Cassie," Kenya said. "She'll come around. She's just a little sensitive."

"That's okay," I said. **"I DON'T MIND."**

Seriously, I didn't mind.

I was just still trying to figure out the whole puberty cow thing. . .

So wrong.

Buried

Kenya went upstairs to get the attic ready for me.

So I just stood next to Kyle for a few minutes.

Then, suddenly, something ran by me, **GRABBED MY LEG** and ran out of the back door.

"What was that?" I asked Kyle.

But Kyle just stood there with his mouth open, pointing at my leg.

"Uh . . . that was Lizzie, our dog," Kyle said, staring at me. "Dude, are you okay?"

"Oh, I'm good. You wouldn't happen to have any spare legs around here, would you?"

Kyle just kept staring at my leg, "Uh . . . I think I'm just going to go find Lizzie."

Then Kyle ran out of the room, really fast.

He was looking a little **GREEN**, too.

I think I'm rubbing off on him.

Yeah, dogs get kind of weird around zombies sometimes.

For some reason, they keep trying to bury us back in the ground.

But the good thing is that Kyle and Kenya didn't have cat.

CATS ARE THE WORST.

It's like they go crazy for the taste of zombie flesh.

So zombies need to be really careful when there are cats around.

Especially when you need to pee. . .

I mean, it's really hard to go pee when you don't have any fingers.

Then Kyle came back in the room with my leg.

Except, it looked like a **LAWN MOWER** ran over it.

"Zombie, what happened to your leg?!!!" Kenya asked, walking downstairs.

Kyle just stood there making noises. "Uhhhhh . . ."

Then Kyle pulled out something called DUCT TAPE and gave Kenya a weird smile.

But I don't think it worked very well.

She just gave him a **MEAN LOOK**.

"Don't worry, Zombie. I'll go by the Zombie Surplus Center later. I heard they've got some new parts in this week. But for now, you can sleep in the living room tonight until we get the attic cleaned up tomorrow."

So then I just hopped behind Kenya into the living room.

When I looked back, Kyle was still standing by the stairs.

He was just standing there . . . **SCRATCHING HIS HEAD**.

The Neighborhood

When I woke up this morning, there was a **BRAND-NEW LEG** by the couch.

And it was a righty, too. Yes!

But when I tried to put it on, there was a big problem.

It was the same length as my left leg!

Aw, man! That meant that I had to walk upright, like a human.

So embarrassing, I know.

HUMAN

ZOMBIE

Now, Kyle and Kenya were busy cleaning up the attic.

And Cassie was still in her room sleeping.

Man, I really wanted to go outside and check out the **NEIGHBORHOOD**.

But I was kind of scared walking out there by myself.

But you know, HumanTown is probably different, I thought.

So, I stepped out the door and into the street.

As I walked a little down the street, people were looking through their windows with their **MOUTHS OPEN** and pointing at me again.

I didn't want to be rude, so I opened my mouth and pointed back.

"Where do you think you're going?" I heard a voice behind me say.

"Yeah, dude. Where do you think you're going?"

I turned around and there were a couple of human kids on bicycles following behind me.

"Hi, my name is Zombie. But you can call me Z."

"PFFFFFFTTTTTTT!!!!!"

The kids just started laughing and pointing at me.

So I started laughing and pointing back.

"This is our neighborhood," the biggest boy said.

"Yeah, so you'd better crawl back to whatever box you came from," another boy said.

"That's a great idea," I said. "Crawling really helps a lot when I get tired. Thanks."

"PFFFFFFTTTTTTT!!!!!"

Then they all started laughing again.

Then, one of the boys put his bicycle on the ground and started to make his hands into fists.

Then the other boys started making fists too.

Whoa, I used to play this game at the zombie village!

The way it works is that the first one to drop a poo wins.

So I just squatted, made my hands into fists, and started building my little log cabin.

"HEY, WHAT'S THE PROBLEM?" I heard a voice say.

All of a sudden, the kids started acting weird as an older boy walked up behind me.

"No, no problem, Steve," the big boy said, trying to get back on his bicycle.

"No problem. Nothing. We're good. Just passing by," all the other kids said.

Then all the kids just jumped on their bicycles and took off.

Man, just when I was about to release the chocolate hostages too.

"Well, at least those guys won't be bothering you anymore," the older boy said. **"WHAT'S YOUR NAME?"**

"My name is Zombie. But you can call me Z."

"Hey, Z, I'm Steve," he said. "Did you just move here?"

"Yeah. I was about to crawl back to the box I came from when you got here."

Steve just stared at me with a **CONFUSED LOOK**.

So I pointed to my house over in the corner.

"Oh, you live with Kyle and Kenya. Yeah, they're cool. You'll really like them."

"What box did you crawl out of?" I asked Steve.

"Uh, I live on the other side of the railroad tracks," Steve said. "There's an old junkyard there where I live with my uncle."

Whoa! A JUNKYARD!

I've heard about those! Junkyards are where humans throw all the things they buy and never use.

"I would really like to visit the junkyard one day," I said. "I heard you can score some sweet merch at a junkyard."

Steve gave me another weird look. But then he said, "Yeah, one day you should come by. But I think Kyle is waving at you. Maybe some other time."

"Sure. I'll see you later, Steve."

So I made my way back to the house.

Wow. He was **REALLY NICE**, I thought.

See. I knew humans were cool.

I think I'm going to really like it here.

When I finally got to the house, Kyle just looked down at me and made a weird face.

"Uhhhh, Zombie, you can come up to the attic to see your new room now."

"Seriously? I have my own room?"

"Yeah. So please get off the ground and come in before the neighbors call the **POLICE**."

Whoa.

For the first time in my life I have **MY OWN ROOM**.

The only time I ever had my own room was when I accidentally locked myself in the outhouse at the zombie village.

Wow. Things can't get any better than this!

My New Room

Kenya brought me up to my new room.

It was amazing!

It had a bed, and it had a lamp.

And there was even a **LITTLE TABLE** with a chair next to it.

"You can put your clothes in here," Kenya said, pointing to a box with handles on it.

"I don't have any clothes," I told her.

"Really, you don't have an extra pair of shirts or pants or underwear?"

"What's **UNDERWEAR**?" I asked her.

Then Kenya just gave me a really weird look.

"This is called a dresser drawer," she said. "You can put your clothes in here when you take a bath."

"What's a bath?" I asked her.

Then she gave me an even weirder look.

"Something tells me I need to disinfect the couch," she muttered.

"What?"

"Err, nothing. . .nothing."

"I really like the little table," I told her.

"Yeah, you can use it to **WRITE** in your diary," she said.

"Actually, I would rather use it to display my collection," I said.

"Really, you have an action figure collection?"

"No, **MY BOOGER COLLECTION**," I said, pulling out my suitcase.

Then Kenya gave me another weird look.

I started thinking I should talk to Kenya about her weird looks.

Old Man Jenkins said that if you make a weird face, and a fly flies by and poops on your face, it'll freeze like that forever.

I was going to tell her. . .

But I think it was **TOO LATE**.

"One more thing," Kenya said. "I have a **SURPRISE** for you."

She pulled out a black bag, and out of the black bag she pulled out her laptop.

"I want you to have it," she said. "I'm getting another one, and I know how much you like watching videos."

Man, I couldn't believe it!

My very **OWN LAPTOP**, in my very own room, on my very own table.

This was the most amazing day of my life.

I was so happy, I ran over and gave Kenya a hug.

I had never given anybody a hug before.

It felt really nice.

Especially when she hugged me back.

And I was really impressed by how she could hug me and hold her breath for **SUCH A LONG TIME**.

Personal Hygiene

I woke up this morning and there was a bucket full of stuff next to my bed, with a big sign next to it that said **"USE ME."**

Inside the bucket was a bunch of stuff I had never seen before.

There was a bottle of something called SHAMPOO.

It said you're supposed to put it on your hair.

And I thought only Zombies put poo in their hair.

So cool.

There was a really big **TOOTHBRUSH** in the bucket too.

There was a sign on it that said it was something called a SCRUB-BRUSH.

It was so big, I thought the person who used this thing must have teeth as big as my head.

Then there was a tube of something called TOOTH-PASTE, which said it goes with something called MOUTH-WASH.

There was also a bottle of something called LO-TION.

And there was a big bar of SO-AP and a thing next to it called a TO-WEL.

Inside the bucket were **INSTRUCTIONS** on how to use everything.

First there were instructions to take something called a "SHO-WER."

So I thought I would read the rest of the instructions while I got in the SHO-WER, to save time.

But then the paper **MELTED**.

Man, what was I supposed to do with all this stuff now?

I was going to call Cassie, but last time she walked in when I was in the bathroom, she started changing colors and acting really weird.

I guess I have to figure it out by myself, I thought.

So, I got out of the SHO-WER, put my clothes on and grabbed the bottle of SHAM-POO.

After reading the instructions, I poured the **WHOLE BOTTLE** on my head.

I didn't think it smelled like poo at all.

But I finally realized the benefits of being a zombie with no eyes.

Then I grabbed the SCRUB-BRUSH and I put the TOOTH-PASTE on it.

But I had a really hard time **FITTING** the brush in my mouth.

I kept pushing and pushing until I finally got it in

But man, I had a really hard time moving it around, though.

I grabbed the bottle of MOUTH-WASH and used the whole thing.

Good thing I had it too.

I was really **THIRSTY**.

The bottle of LO-TION said I needed to use it on my hands and my face.

So I opened it up and poured it all over my face.

It kind of felt like the **VOMIT BATHS** I used to take at the zombie village.

But it didn't smell as good.

I didn't know what to do with the bucket, so I just put it on my head.

I saw a picture of a zombie do that once, and I thought it looked so cool.

Copyright PVZ 2019

I was actually **PRETTY PROUD** of myself.

And I couldn't wait to show the world how good I looked, too.

But Kyle said I should probably stay indoors.

He said something about the neighbors calling the police again.

Humans . . . So weird.

The Play Date

Today Kenya told me that one of our neighbors invited us over for something called a PLAY-DATE.

Kenya said her neighbor had a boy my age who was having trouble **MAKING FRIENDS**.

She said since we were the same age, we might just have some things in common.

Now, I didn't really know what to do.

Nobody had ever invited me over for a PLAY-DATE before.

So I said yes.

Sometimes, you just have to **LIVE ON THE EDGE**, you know.

The neighbors lived just a few blocks away from us.

When we got to their house, it looked just like Kyle and Kenya's.

Then Kenya knocked on the door.

We stood there for a little while and then a really nice lady answered.

"Hi, Kenya, it's great to see you," she said. Then she looked at me. "And who might you be?"

"Hi. My name is Zombie. But you can call me Z."

"Well, hi, Z. It's great to meet you. My name is Ms. Rachel. And I would like to introduce you to **MY SON** . . . uh . . . Now, where did he run to?"

Ms. Rachel said that her son was in the house somewhere.

But I started thinking that maybe she made him up.

I saw on YouTube once that people make up imaginary friends when they feel lonely.

And Kenya said Ms. Rachel was a **SINGLE MOM**.

So it kind of made sense.

"There you are. Come over here and meet your new neighbor," she said.

All of a sudden, a kid walked out of the bathroom.

He was skinny, had a round head and he had red bumps and holes all over his face.

He kind of looked like a zombie, but pink.

"Hey," the boy said.

"Hey. I'm Zombie. But you can call me Z."

"Hey, Z, I'm Franklin," he said.

But when he smiled, I was totally blown away.

I had never seen a human with **METAL TEETH** before.

"Why don't you two go play in Franklin's room while Kenya and I catch up," Ms. Rachel said.

"Okay," we both said. Then we ran upstairs to Franklin's room.

As soon as we got to his room, Franklin closed and locked the door. CLICK!

"Hey, Z, do you like **GAMES**?" Franklin asked me.

"I sure do. We used to play all kind of games at my zombie village. My favorite game was Twister. Except for some reason, we only played it once . . . and only for a few minutes."

CRACK

"Do you want to play my favorite game?" Franklin asked, with a really weird smile on his face.

"Sure, what is it?"

"I call it **'FIND MY BELLY BUTTON,'**" Franklin said.

"Wait. . .what?"

"Wanna play?" he asked me again.

"Uhhhh. . .sure."

But then I started getting this weird feeling that something was just not right with this situation.

Then Franklin lifted his shirt up, and I noticed something **WEIRD**.

"Whoa. Where's your belly button?" I asked him.

"I don't know. The doctor said that I must have one, but no one knows where it is."

I just stood there, a bit confused.

"So. . .you ready to play?" Franklin asked.

"Uhhhhh . . ."

"Boys!" I heard Ms. Rachel yell. "We have some snacks downstairs. Come down and get some!"

I don't know why, but something told me I had just **DODGED A BULLET**.

So we both ran down the stairs to the kitchen.

And it was awesome!

Ms. Rachel had all kinds of snacks.

She had chips, candy, and cookies.

But then I saw my favorite snack in the whole world, **CAKE**!

"Z, have as much cake as you want," Ms. Rachel said. "And here, Franklin, I made some brownie rolls just for you."

She passed Franklin a huge plate full of brownies that were shaped like hot dogs.

Then Franklin started eating them like he had never eaten before.

It's like, he would put them near his face and they would just **DISAPPEAR**.

Then Ms. Rachel and Kenya went into the other room to finish talking.

I tried to eat faster so I could show Franklin that I was **THE FASTEST**.

But no matter how fast I ate, Franklin would just inhale his brownie rolls without even chewing.

Finally, after a few minutes, we were tied.

We were just a few pieces of cake and a few brownie rolls away from calling the winner.

Then Ms. Rachel and Kenya came into the kitchen.

"Oh dear!" Ms. Rachel said.

We had eaten so fast, there was cake and brownie rolls all over the place.

"Sorry, Ms. Rachel. We'll clean it up," I said.

But then Franklin started **LAUGHING**.

"PFFFFFFTTTTTT!!!!"

Franklin laughed so hard that brownies started shooting out of his nose.

"Oh dear!" Ms. Rachel said again, as she and Kenya tried to avoid getting sprayed.

Then Ms. Rachel rushed Franklin to the bathroom.

Me and Kenya stayed behind so that we could **CLEAN THE KITCHEN**.

It was a lot of work.

And I'm pretty sure we got most of it.

But there was no way we could get the brown and green spots **OFF THE CEILING**.

Ms. Rachel and Franklin were in the bathroom for long time.

So me and Kenya decided to leave quietly.

You know, even though it was a little weird, I had fun.

Wow. Who knows, maybe Franklin could be my **NEW BEST FRIEND**.

I think I can even get used to his funny smell.

The Fire Brigade

Today, Kyle asked me if I wanted to go visit where he works.

"What's a **FIRE BRIGADE?**" I asked him.

"That's the name of a group of people that fight fires for a living," he said.

It sounded really cool, so I said yes.

When we got to Kyle's job, it was amazing.

And they had all kinds of cool things there too.

They had these huge hoses that looked like **GIANT SNAKES**.

And they had these huge yellow pants and coats you could put on and walk around in.

They even had these huge red buckets on the table that you could spit into.

I think Kyle called them HEL-METS.

What was cool is that I think I broke my record for the **BIGGEST LOOGIE** I ever hocked.

HEL-METS . . . so cool.

And they also had the coolest red fire truck ever.

I had to try it, so I climbed on top and acted like I was a **FIREFIGHTER**.

"What in tarnation are you doing up there?" I heard a voice from inside the fire truck say.

Then a huge green head full of boils, brown spots, and white hair came out from inside the fire truck.

"Mr. Jenkins! What are you doing here?!!!"

"Hey there, Zombie," Old Man Jenkins said.

"Mr. Jenkins works for me now," Kyle said. "He and his assistants just started a few days ago. They keep the place clean for us while we're out fighting fires."

"What assistants?"

"Hey, Zombie!" one voice said.

"'Sup, Zombie!" another voice said.

"What's crackin', Zombie?!!!" a third voice said.

NED! ZED! FRED! You guys are here too?"

"Yep, we're working for the fire brigade now," Ned said.

"We're heroes!" Zed said.

"READY FOR BATTLE!" Fred said.

"Whoa. Hold on there, fellas," Kyle said. "Remember, you guys are here to just keep the place clean and organized. You need to leave the firefighting to us humans, okay?"

"Don't worry, Mr. Kyle," Old Man Jenkins said. "I'll make sure they don't cause any trouble."

But I could tell the guys didn't really like that.

"Not fair," Ned muttered.

"So sad," Zed stuttered.

"Bum rap," Fred duttered.

"You guys are heroes to me," I whispered.

That made them really **HAPPY**, so they went back to cleaning the fire station.

"Wow, you really fight fires?" I asked Kyle. "What's it like?"

"Well, it's cool, but really dangerous. We have to be extra careful to make sure nobody gets hurt. That's why we use all this equipment."

Wow. This so cool, I thought.

Then, suddenly, a **BELL** started ringing.

RRRRRRIIIINNNGGGG!!!!!

Old Man Jenkins and the guys started helping hand out equipment.

Then a group of humans put on their yellow uniforms, grabbed their equipment and jumped on the fire truck.

Kyle double checked all the equipment to make sure it was okay, and then he grabbed a HEL-MET and jumped on the fire truck.

"Zombie, I'll be back in a little while to take you home," he said.

I waved **GOODBYE** as the fire truck raced away.

Kyle started waving back, but then he just gave me the strangest look.

Whoa, being on the fire brigade is so **COOL**, I thought.

It's too bad that zombies aren't allowed to do it.

Getting Adjusted

Well, it's been a few weeks since I moved into HumanTown.

And I think I am finally getting **ADJUSTED**.

But I still don't totally understand humans.

Like, a few days ago, I found some lice in my hair.

I was so excited, I ran over to Cassie's room to tell her.

She wasn't there, so I decided to leave some on her pillow.

You know . . . to show her how much I **APPRECIATE** her.

Then, a few days later, I heard a lot of yelling and screaming coming from her room.

So I was really glad to hear she liked them.

I went over to her room to ask her if she wanted some more.

But then her eye started **TWITCHING**, and she slammed the door.

Like I said . . . weird.

And for some reason, Kenya keeps buying me new underwear.

But I really didn't know what to do with them.

She told me that I had to change my underwear every day.

But I didn't really get that.

I mean, I really didn't understand how you could attract flies that way.

Especially the pregnant ones that lay eggs.

She said she brought me **SEVEN PAIR OF UNDERWEAR** so I could use one every day.

She said I could use one for every day of the week.

Like one for Monday, Tuesday, Wednesday . . .

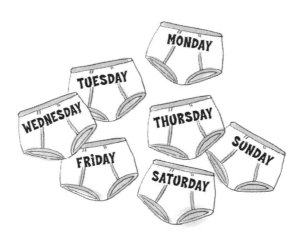

But I asked her to buy me **TWELVE** instead.

That made her really happy.

I mean, it kind of makes more sense to me.

You know, one for January, February, March . . .

My booger collection is getting bigger every day, though.

I even made a whole jar of ZOMBIE JAM out of it.

What's ZOMBIE JAM?

Well, it's like the most **VERSATILE SUBSTANCE** on earth.

Kind of like DUCT TAPE, but for zombies.

In case you wanted to know what **ZOMBIE JAM** is made of, I have a list right here . . .

ZOMBIE JAM
FAMILY RECIPE

Boogers
Ear Wax
Toe Jam
Snot
Dandruff
Spit
Pimple Juice
Nose Hairs

Belly Button cheese

Fresh Scabs
and some
flaky feet
skins

ZOMBIE JAM comes in really handy, too.

Like the other day, Kyle's desk lamp broke.

So I used a whole jar of ZOMBIE JAM and made him a really big scented candle to use in his office.

I even added some fresh **NOSE MAGGOTS** so it would be nice and meaty.

So now, whenever Kyle needs some light, he can enjoy the sweet aroma of ZOMBIE JAM while he's working.

When I gave it to him, he gave me a weird smile and closed the door to his office.

But I could tell he totally loved it, though.

I could hear him jumping up and down and **SCREAMING FOR JOY** behind the door.

The Pool Party

Today one of Cassie's friends invited her to something called a POOL PARTY.

I didn't know what a pool party was until I asked Kenya.

What I didn't know was what Kenya was going to say next.

"Hey, Cassie, why don't you take Zombie with you?" Kenya said. "It will be a great chance for him to make **NEW FRIENDS**."

Let's just say that when Cassie heard that, I was really scared she was going to give birth to another cow.

Then, Kenya thought it would be a good idea to invite Franklin too.

Yeah, forget the cow.

We probably need to make room for a **BABY DINOSAUR** instead.

Cassie couldn't do much about it, though.

That's because she needed Kenya to drive her to the POOL PARTY.

So Cassie finally said yes. Except now, every time Cassie looks at me, her eyes turn **BLOOD RED** and I hear claps of thunder in the background.

Now, I didn't really know what to wear to a POOL PARTY.

Kenya just told me to wear something called TRUNKS.

So I went to my room to get ready.

But then Kenya walked in my room and didn't say anything for a few minutes.

Then she walked out.

But I really wish TRUNKS were more like underwear.

Especially since underwear are so much **LIGHTER**.

We picked up Franklin in our car and drove to the party.

But Cassie kept yelling for us to roll down the window.

I really didn't understand why.

She must not like the smell of brownie rolls, I guess.

When we got to the party, there were a bunch of kids splashing around in the pool.

I had never seen so many **PINK AND BROWN** bodies in one place before.

Then Kenya told me to go to the bathroom and change into my TRUNKS.

But I decided to wear shorts instead.

That's because the TRUNKS were really drafty around my nether regions.

WOOOOOH, SO COLD.

Kenya said she would pick us up in a few hours, and she left.

And as soon as Kenya drove away, Cassie disappeared into the sea of skinny bodies.

Franklin already had his shorts on, so he just jumped in the pool with the other kids.

As for me, I went to the bathroom to change my clothes.

But then, I started feeling a little **SELF-CONSCIOUS**.

What if the kids don't like me? I thought.

I mean, I'm not pink. . .or brown. What if they don't like my green skin?

Well, at least I've got one thing going for me.

Yeah . . . they won't be able to resist these legs.

But I was still really nervous, so I decided to stay in the bathroom for a while.

Then, after a few minutes, I finally got the **COURAGE** to go outside.

But when I walked out of the bathroom, I noticed something really weird . . .

All the kids were gone.

The only one left in the pool was Franklin.

And he was just sitting there, chillin', snacking on some brownie rolls.

So me and Franklin spent the whole afternoon playing in the pool **ALL BY OURSELVES**.

It was awesome.

But when I got home, Kenya told me that Cassie didn't have such a good time at the party.

You know, I still can't figure out why . . .

The Sleepover

"Mom, we're still having my sleepover tonight, right?" Cassie asked.

"Honey, can we do it another day?" Kenya said. "With Zombie staying with us, and Kyle's annual work party tonight, there's a lot going on."

Then Cassie gave me a mean look.

And my **FOREHEAD** started getting really hot for some reason.

"Mom! You promised! I've been waiting all month to have my friends over! That's not fair!"

She kept yelling for about five minutes, and then she started **THROWING HERSELF** on the floor too.

"Okay! Okay! Please stop having a meltdown!" Kenya said.

Cassie got up off the ground and gave me a smile.

Then she skipped up to her room and slammed the door.

"Zombie, Cassie is having a sleepover tonight," Kenya told me. "And Kyle and I are going to be home late because of his work party."

"Okay," I said, not really knowing what was going on.

"Are you going to be okay by yourself?"

"Sure."

"I HAVE AN IDEA," Kenya continued. "Why don't you invite Franklin to sleep over tonight too? That way you won't feel weird being around a bunch of teenage girls. And Ms. Rachel can come out with us tonight. I think she needs a night out."

"Uh. . .sure."

"Okay, great. I'll call Ms. Rachel and tell her to bring Franklin over around six-thirty," Kenya said. "I think all of you are going to have a night you will **NEVER FORGET**."

Even though I didn't really understand what was going on, something told me that she was probably right.

The Sleepover,
Later That Night . . .

DING-DONG!

"Zombie, can you get the door please?" Kenya
yelled. "It's probably Cassie's friends."

So I went to the door and opened it.

Next thing I know, a bunch of girls ran into the house.

"WHO ARE YOU?" one of them asked.

"Where did you come from?" another one asked.

"Where's Cassie?" a third girl said.

"Where's the food?" a fourth girl said.

"It smells like bacon. Oooh, I love bacon!" a big girl said.

Then Cassie ran downstairs to the group of giggling girls.

"WHO'S THE STIFF?"

"Oh, that's Zombie. He's staying with us for a while," Cassie said.

"Whoa, he's a real zombie?" one of the girls asked. Then the rest of them got really close and started looking me over.

"Does he talk? What does he eat? Why does he smell like bacon? Do zombies poop?"

I didn't know what to do so I just stood there making zombie noises.

"URRRRGGGGHHHH . . ."

"Whoa! Do it again! Do it again!"

Next thing I know, Cassie started making zombie noises too.

"Urgh! Forget about him! Let's go to the living room and paint our toenails," she said.

Then the giggling girls went to the living room.

Except the big girl smacked me on the butt on the way out.

SO WEIRD.

I really didn't know what just happened.

So I just went to the kitchen to get some snacks.

DING-DONG!

"Can someone get the door?" Kenya yelled from upstairs again. "I'm still getting ready."

Then me and Cassie reached the door together.

"Hi, Cassie. Hi, Zombie," Ms. Rachel said. "Franklin is here for the sleepover."

"**WHAT?!!!!**" Cassie said as her eye started twitching again.

Just then, Kenya and Kyle walked down the stairs.

"Hey, Rachel, perfect timing," Kenya said. "Cassie, you're in charge. So please make sure you take care of Zombie and Franklin while we're out, okay?"

Then Cassie started turning a weird **SHADE OF RED**.

"Okay, goodbye, kids. Have fun," Kenya said as they walked out the door.

Cassie just stood there without moving, getting redder and redder.

Next thing I know, she **SLAMMED** the door.

"Listen, you little Cretan. You and your creepy friend better not bother me and my friends tonight, or you're going to be sorry, okay?!!!"

"Uh . . . sure," I said, still not really knowing what was going on.

Then she stomped into the other room.

I looked over at Franklin, and he looked like he was about to faint.

"ISN'T SHE BEAUTIFUL?" Franklin said.

The Sleepover, Even Later That Night . . .

After a few hours it started getting dark outside.

Me and Franklin just passed the time making a whole new jar of ZOMBIE JAM.

I've got to admit, I didn't think Franklin would contribute much.

But he totally **REPRESENTED**.

He had like an endless supply of ingredients.

So cool.

At the end, we had so much ZOMBIE JAM that we decided to make the biggest castle ever.

"Let's start our castle," I said.

But I could tell that Franklin really wanted to go see what the girls were doing.

So we decided to **SNEAK** downstairs.

When we got into the living room, we noticed the girls were watching a movie.

They were jumping and screaming every few minutes, so I think it was a scary movie.

"Isn't she pretty?" Franklin kept saying.

"Uhhhh . . . Franklin, I think Cassie is going to get mad if she sees us standing here staring at her all night."

So we decided to just go to the kitchen to get some **SNACKS**.

"Want to hear me make words with my farts?" Franklin asked me.

"What?"

"Want to hear me make words with my farts?" he asked again.

"Uhhh . . . okay."

Franklin put on a weird face and then . . .

"FFFAAAARRRRRRTTTTT!!!!"

Whoa.

I didn't know what to say.

I had never heard somebody's butt speak before.

"Want me to do it again?"

"FFFAAAARRRRRTTTTT!!!!"

"Want me to say another word?"

"Uh . . . sure?"

"HHHHEEEEYYYYY!!!!!"

"I can make it really loud, too," Franklin said.

139

Then he clenched his butt cheeks real tight and started sweating.

All of a sudden . . .

WWWWHHHAAAATTTT!!!!

It was so loud, a car alarm went off next door.

"WWWHHHAAAAATTTTT!!!!!"

He did it again. Except, this time it was so loud, it made my insides move.

"WWWHHHAAAAATTTTT!!!!!"

Then, all of a sudden . . .

PLOP!

Uh-oh.

I think Franklin had an accident.

Or, he might need a **NEW KIDNEY**.

Then Franklin started laughing, and chips and milk started shooting out of his nose again.

DING-DONG!

Then I heard somebody at the front door.

I was really hoping it wasn't Kenya.

The kitchen was totally covered in creamy chips and orange milk.

When I went to the door, I noticed Cassie and her friends weren't in the living room anymore.

I guess they went upstairs to Cassie's bedroom, I thought.

DING-DONG!

Then I opened the door.

"COME OUT OF THE HOUSE WITH YOUR HANDS UP!" I heard somebody yell.

Then there were **FLASHING LIGHTS AND SIRENS** everywhere.

"PLEASE, SIR, MAKE THIS EASY ON YOURSELF. COME OUT OF THE HOUSE, GET ON THE GROUND AND PUT YOUR HANDS BEHIND YOUR HEAD!"

So I just did what the angry man said.

"Officer, **IT'S NOT HIM**," I heard Cassie say. "He's staying with us."

143

"What exactly did you hear, ma'am?" the man in the blue uniform asked her.

"It sounded like a **MONSTER**," Cassie said.

"It had a really deep voice," one of Cassie's friends said.

"It sounded big, like a gorilla!" another one of Cassie's friends said."

"And it said, 'WWWWHHHHAAATTTTT!!!!'" the big girl said. ". . .Like it wanted to eat us!"

The man in the blue uniform just stood there scratching his head.

Then he and a few other uniformed men went inside.

Then, after a little while, they all ran out **REALLY FAST**.

"Don't go in there!" the man said. "It's horrible! Whatever it was, it left a pair of pants, and some brown, orange and white sauce all over the floor!"

Just then, Kenya, Kyle and Ms. Rachel pulled up in their car.

"You were very **LUCKY** tonight," the uniformed man said to Cassie and her friends.

Then he walked over to the people with cameras. "Well, ladies and gentlemen, it seems like we have some type of wild animal on the loose . . . please keep your children and pets inside tonight."

Kenya, Kyle, and Ms. Rachel just stood there wondering what just happened.

The next day, the TV said that there was a wild and vicious animal loose in our area.

Some people said it may have been the CHUPA-CABRA.

A few people even said they had seen it.

They said it had **METAL TEETH**, it was drooling, and it was wearing a shirt with no pants.

Anyway, I asked Kenya to call Ms. Rachel to see if Franklin was okay.

I hadn't seen him since the sleepover.

But she said that Ms. Rachel and Franklin went **OUT OF TOWN** for a few days.

She said something about them having to lay low until the heat died down.

I didn't get it.

It didn't really seem that hot to me.

Like I said . . .

Humans . . . so weird.

AUGUST

An Invitation to Dinner

Today I got the weirdest invitation.

Somebody came by the house in a big black car and gave Kenya a **LETTER**.

The letter said I was invited to the mayor's house for dinner.

It said that the town council wanted to welcome the first zombie ever to live in HumanTown, and the mayor wanted to meet me personally.

Whoa. I had never been invited to **DINNER** before.

But Kenya said that a lot of important people from all over HumanTown were going to be there, so I should go.

I didn't really know what all that meant.

But she said there would be nuggets and cake, so I said yes.

Kenya said that I had to wear something nice to the dinner.

So she asked me if I had anything nice to **WEAR**.

I looked through my drawers, but the only new thing I had were underwear. So, I showed her and Kyle what I had.

Kyle told me he was going to get me something called a TUX-EDO instead.

Then he told me to put my clothes back on because the neighbors were probably going to call the police.

Then I started getting a little nervous.

I mean, I had never been to a dinner before.

"What do I do when I get to the dinner?" I asked Kyle. "I mean, how am I supposed to act?"

"Just do what everybody else does, and you'll fit in fine," Kyle said.

It sounded like a **GOOD IDEA**, and that made me feel a lot better.

Later, Kyle came back with a tuxedo.

He said he got it from Good Will, so it might be a little old.

But I was so happy, that I really didn't care hold old Will was.

So then I put on the **TUXEDO**.

I had never worn a tuxedo before, and it felt really weird.

Especially because the little needles sticking in my skin made the tuxedo really itchy.

But it made Kenya really happy, so I didn't mind.

"Zombie, you look great," Kenya said. "I'm so proud of you."

Then Kenya started **TEARING UP**.

I didn't really know what to do, so I just gave her a hug.

I went to give Kyle a hug too, but I think he said he got something in his eye. Because he ran into the bathroom and locked the door.

A Piece of Advice

Later, I went outside to watch the sweaty guys playing with the lawn.

"Nice tux," I heard somebody say.

"Oh, hey, Steve!" I said.

"What's the **SPECIAL OCCASION**?" Steve asked me.

"Well, I got invited to the mayor's house. They said that since I was the first zombie in HumanTown, they wanted to meet me in person."

Then Steve gave me a look.

"Hey, you need to be careful around here, Zombie," Steve said.

"Really, why?"

"Well, sometimes people don't like people that are **DIFFERENT** than they are," he said. "And even though they can be nice on the outside, they can also be really slimy on the inside."

"Oh, you mean like dung beetles? Yeah. But you get used to it after a few bites."

Steve gave me a weird look again.

"Hey, remember you don't have to be like everybody else. You just need to be who you are, green skin, warts and all."

Then Steve gave me a fist pound.

"Stay true to yourself, man!" Steve said as he walked away.

Didn't Kyle just tell me I should try to **FIT IN**? I thought, feeling a little confused.

But you know, Steve did have a point.

I mean, it would be so much easier to be myself.

And I really didn't like wearing the tuxedo.

So I sat down and started thinking a lot about what Steve said.

Then I heard a voice behind me.

"Hey, Zombie. What are you doing outside **DRESSED** like that?"

When I looked up, it was Old Man Jenkins walking by.

"Oh, hey, Mr. Jenkins."

"Zombie, you look like a penguin about to fart a hamster."

"Oh, I was just sitting here, **THINKING** about something," I said.

"Well, don't hurt yourself. Zombies aren't wired to do much thinkin'. It's kinda' hard when its hollow upstairs, you know."

"Uhh . . . sure. Um . . . Mr. Jenkins, can I ask you a question?"

"Sure thing, Zombie. I'm all ears."

I felt really sad for a minute.

But I really didn't have much time to help Mr. Jenkins with his ears.

"Um . . . Mr. Jenkins, should I be more like humans, so I could fit in? Or should I just, you know . . . be myself?"

"Well, Zombie, that's a **PICKLE**. I would even say it's a question that's dumbfounded people for centuries."

"Uh . . . huh . . ."

"But you know what I think? I think because you're different that makes you special. And people always like things that are special."

Whoa, that was so deep.

I really didn't understand it, but it was deep.

"Thanks, Mr. Jenkins," I said.

Then I ran back in the house.

So, I've made up my mind.

When I get to the mayor's house, I'm just going to be **MYSELF**.

And like Mr. Jenkins said, the more special I am, the more they're going to totally like me.

So look out, Mayor, cause here I come!

Getting Ready

Today was the dinner at the mayor's house.

The bad news is that Kenya **GOT SICK**, so she couldn't come.

But Kyle said he would meet me there after his shift at the fire station.

The good news was that since HumanTown was a such small town, the mayor's house wasn't that far away.

So, I decided to walk.

On the way there, I thought it would be a great opportunity for me to prepare my special zombie self.

So the first thing I did was to make sure I **SMELLED** right.

There was a pig farm in town, so I decided to kick it with the pigs for a little while.

One thing I love about pigs is that out of all the different animals, they smell the closest to what zombies smell like.

And I made sure to rub some cow pies on me too, to add a bit more zest to the mix.

My breath was only a little **STINKY** because I didn't brush my teeth this morning.

So I decided to spice it up with a little help from some stinky socks I was saving for a rainy day.

My tuxedo didn't have enough holes in it, so I tore a few more.

And what really topped it off was a nice infestation of maggots in my hair, ears, and clothes.

I had a bunch left over, so I just kept the rest in my pocket.

And I also packed a plastic baggy with some **BOOGER SNACKS** in case I got hungry on the way.

Aaahhh. I felt great. Just like my old self again.

But then, on my way to the mayor's house, I got lost.

I tried to ask for **DIRECTIONS**.

But every time I walked up to somebody, they just screamed and ran the other way for some reason.

Then I saw a lot of people getting on something called the BUS.

So I hopped on the BUS to see if anybody there could give me directions.

But it was really hard talking to people.

Especially when they were so busy trying to climb out the windows.

Like I said . . .

Humans . . . **SO WEIRD**.

Dinner at the Mayor's House

When I finally found the **MAYOR'S HOUSE**, I was totally blown away.

It was the biggest house I had ever seen.

I knocked on the door and a guy called a WAIT-OR answered the door.

When I started telling him my name, he just ran away holding his mouth.

It's like he had a bug that was trying to crawl out or something.

But I totally get it.

That happens to me whenever the **TAPEWORMS** in my stomach grow too big.

I even walk around and act like I have a really long tongue when they start coming out.

So fun.

I went into the house, and after walking around for a few minutes, I got lost again.

"Are you lost?" I heard a girl's voice behind me say.

But when I turned around, suddenly, I couldn't move.

I just stood there, making zombie noises.

"URRRRGHHHH . . ."

"Hi, I'm Beverly," the girl said. "I live here. Are you here for the party?"

"URRRRGHHHH . . ."

Then the weirdest feeling came over me.

All I could do was stand there and drool.

"URRRRGHHHH . . ."

"Well, the dining room is that way," she said. "I'm going to my room now, okay?"

Then she floated away on a cloud, into her room.

That was weird.

I've never felt that way before.

It's like the room got hot and cold at the same time.

It felt like I had the biggest butterflies in my stomach.

And I don't think it was because of all those **CATERPILLARS** I ate.

Anyway, I finally found the dining room.

As soon as I walked in, I saw a bunch of people wearing tuxedos and dresses.

And when they saw me, everybody just opened their mouths and started pointing again.

So I said hi back.

I saw an **EMPTY SEAT** next to the main table, so I sat down in it.

It was actually the seat right next to the mayor.

She seemed like a really nice lady.

So I pulled my hand out of my pocket to shake hands with the her, but I forgot I had a pocket full of maggots.

"Oops. Sorry about that. I forgot I had some extra maggots in my pocket. Does anybody want some?"

Then everybody at the table started changing **COLORS**.

One lady turned blue. Another man turned purple. One guy turned really white. And another lady turned green.

I didn't even know humans could change colors like that.

So cool.

"Hors d'oeuvres, sir?" asked another WAIT-OR, while covering his nose.

Whoa! They looked like little **WIENERS** with coats.

Normally, I only eat nuggets, but the waiter started turning purple, so I stuffed a few into my mouth.

But then, a few minutes later. . .

GRRRRRRRRR!

People started looking around to see where the noise was coming from.

Somebody even said that it sounded like a train passed by.

I guess my stomach really didn't like the wieners.

So I quietly stepped out of the room to see if I could find the bathroom.

But after looking for the bathroom for a while, I got lost again.

All I could find was something called the COAT-CLOSET.

And since I was really ground-hogging it, I just ran into the COAT-CLOSET.

Then I started looking for a box or something I could do my duty in.

But there wasn't anything around except coats.

But then I remembered, **MY PLASTIC BAGGY!**

I was totally saved by my plastic bag of booger snacks.

So I emptied the little plastic baggy out and filled it with some gorilla fingers.

And after I finished, I just stuffed the fat plastic baggy back in my pocket.

When I got back to the dining room, I noticed they were serving **DINNER**.

So I snuck back in and sat in my seat next to the mayor.

"Excuse me, Ms. Mayor lady?"

"Yes, young man, how can I help you?" she asked.

"Could you take care of this for me?" I asked her, as I handed her the warm package.

Suddenly, the mayor lady's eye started twitching . . .

Then she started turning a weird shade of green . . .

Then, next thing I know . . .

BLECH!

SPLAT!

Then, all of a sudden . . . Everybody at the table started puking.

What was really cool was how they puked one right after the other, all around the table.

Kind of reminded me of the Zombie Wave we used to do at baseball games.

I felt like I was back home at the zombie village.

SO COOL.

Kyle was running a little late, but he finally made it toward the end of dinner.

But by the time he got there, for some reason, everybody was sleeping on the table, under the table, or on the floor.

As for me, I was just having fun making **VOMIT ANGELS** on the floor.

. . . Next to the mayor lady.

. . . while she slept.

Kyle's eyes got really big and his mouth dropped open.

Then he **SMACKED** himself really hard on the forehead.

Yeah, I think he was really sad he missed all the fun.

On the way home, Kenya called us to ask what happened.

She said that half of the town was **HYSTERICAL** because of what happened at the mayor's house.

I told her that I decided to "be myself." And it worked out great!

"Uh, Zombie . . ." Kenya said.

"Yeah, Kenya?"

"Never mind . . ." she said as she closed the phone.

Wow, I'm finally starting to fit in around here.

Sweet.

Letter from the Mayor

Today another black car from the mayor's office came by our house.

And they brought another **LETTER**. But this time it wasn't an invitation.

This is what it said:

From the Office of the Mayor of HumanTown:

Due to recent disturbing circumstances, we, the Town Board of HumanTown, have decided that it may not be in the best interest of the residents of our town to have zombies living in our community.

We have therefore set a meeting to decide on adding a new "No Zombie Law" in our town. The law, if approved, will take effect immediately.

This means anyone harboring zombies must either relocate their zombie to the nearest zombie village, or relocate to another town.

The meeting will be held tomorrow night at the Town Hall.

Sincerely,

Mayor Tublerina Thightanic

I didn't really understand what the letter said.

Then Kenya tried explaining it to me.

"It's not that they don't like you, Zombie," she said. "It's just that people are **AFRAID** of things that they don't understand."

Wow, that Steve kind of said too.

"Don't worry, Zombie," Kyle said. "We're going to fight this. We're all going to be there to back you up.

"And I'm going to tell everybody I know to come and let them know what a **GREAT PERSON** you are," Kenya said.

"Except for Cassie," Kyle said.

"Oh, right," Kenya said. "Cassie stays home."

Hmm. So people are afraid because they don't **UNDERSTAND** zombies?

So, I started thinking . . .

What if I help them totally understand everything about zombies?

Then they totally won't be afraid of zombies anymore!

So I decided that I was going to put together the best presentation about zombies, ever.

This **PRESENTATION** is going to totally help everybody understand everything there is to know about zombies, I thought.

And after I'm finished, they're totally going to love us!

Meeting at the Town Hall

I stayed up all night putting together my presentation for tonight's meeting at the Town Hall.

I collected all the information I could find on zombies.

I collected all my notes, diagrams, files, and more.

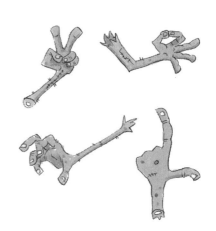

I even had some **OLD ZOMBIE PARTS** for visual aids.

DING-DONG!

I went to the door to see who it was.

"Oh hi, Mr. Jenkins."

"Hey, Zombie," Old Man Jenkins said.

"Hey, Mr. Jenkins, can I ask you some questions? I'm putting together a presentation and . . ."

"Uh . . . sorry, Zombie, but I really need to speak to Mr. Kyle."

Then Old Man Jenkins gave us some **BAD NEWS**.

"Sorry, Mr. Kyle. It seems that the fire brigade decided it didn't want zombies to work at the fire station anymore. I don't understand. Did we do something wrong?"

Then I could see Kyle get really mad.

"Don't worry, Mr. Jenkins," Kyle said. "I'm going to fix this tonight at the town meeting. You'll see. By tomorrow morning, this will just be one big **MISUNDERSTANDING**."

"Thanks, Mr. Kyle," Mr. Jenkins said.

I decided to walk Mr. Jenkins out the door.

Then I told him about the letter.

"Well, I'll be," he said. "That would explain everything."

So then I told Old Man Jenkins about my presentation and how I was going to help everybody understand who zombies really are.

"It would be really great if you could be there," I told him. "I need a few more visual aids. And I think You, Ned, Zed and Fred would be perfect for the **ENTERTAINMENT** portion."

"That sounds like a great idea," he said. "If you think it'll work."

"Oh, yeah. This will totally win them over!" I said.

So, now I am all ready for the meeting.

We are going to **DAZZLE** the mayor and everybody at the Town Hall tonight.

Man, I can't wait!

Trouble in HumanTown

When we got to the meeting, a lot of people from town were there.

But for some reason, they all sat on the **RIGHT SIDE** of the auditorium.

And they made me, Kenya, and Kyle sit on the left.

Ms. Rachel, Franklin, and Steve sat with us too.

Then somebody set up a table of scented candles between us.

I think somebody said something about there being a funny smell.

It kind of made sense, though.

Franklin was a bit more **RIPE** than usual today.

I was really hoping that Old Man Jenkins would be there soon.

I really needed him to help me appeal to the elderly demographic.

But then the meeting started. The first person to speak was the mayor.

She got up and shared her thoughts on the **ZOMBIE PROBLEM**.

Then a lot of other people got up and shared their thoughts on the zombie problem.

And then more people got up and shared about the zombie problem.

Wow. I didn't even know zombies had so many problems.

The meeting went on for a while.

But I didn't mind. I was just really **EXCITED** about my presentation.

Then, all of a sudden, I couldn't believe my eyes!

Beverly was there, sitting right next to the mayor.

She even waved to me.

I didn't know what to do, so I just drooled and made zombie noises.

"URRRRGHHHH . . ."

Then it was our turn to talk about zombies and their problems.

Kenya got up and shared how proud she was to have me as part of her family. She said that the fact that I was a zombie didn't matter because I had such a big heart.

What she said was really nice.

But I probably have to break the bad news to her about **MY HEART**.

Let's just say I had a bad case of explosive diarrhea a few years ago.

Haven't seen my heart since . . .

Then Kyle got up and spoke about how much Old Man Jenkins and Ned, Zed and Fred helped the fire brigade.

Ms. Rachel got up and spoke about Franklin, and how after so many years, he finally found a friend.

And just when I thought everybody was done, Cassie got up and said some really **NICE THINGS** about what it's like living with a zombie.

I didn't hear much of what she said, though.

Because I was still just sitting there, drooling and thinking about Beverly.

Then something **INTERRUPTED** me mid-drool.

"Zombie . . . Zombie . . . Zombie!"

195

"Urrggghhhwuuzzaat?"

"Zombie, it's **YOUR TURN** to give your presentation," Kenya said.

"Oh, yeah, okay."

I was a little nervous and really excited at the same time.

But then I saw Old Man Jenkins, Ned, Zed and Fred walk in through the back door.

Old Man Jenkins gave me a nod, so I knew I was ready.

After I put all my presentation materials up, I asked the people to **DIM THE LIGHTS** for added effect.

So they started dimming the lights and blowing out the candles.

But then, suddenly. . .

KRESH!

Somebody knocked over the table with all the scented candles on it.

Then, next thing we know, a **HUGE FIRE** started in the auditorium.

"Everybody, move out of the way!" Kyle yelled.

Everybody was yelling for the door.

But the door was covered by fire, so nobody could reach it.

Then somebody yelled to go to the **BACK DOOR**.

But the fire had spread, so it blocked the back door too.

Kyle yelled for everybody to move to the front of auditorium because it was the safest place.

But the fire kept growing **BIGGER AND BIGGER**.

And nobody knew what to do . . .

Fireproof!

Then Old Man Jenkins grabbed Kyle.

"Mr. Kyle, we can help!" he said. "Me, Ned, Zed, and Fred can get that door open again!"

"But it's too **DANGEROUS**!" Kyle said.

"Don't worry about us!" Old Man Jenkins yelled. "We were born for this!"

Then Old Man Jenkins, Ned, Zed and Fred ran into the fire, toward the door.

Everybody started screaming and yelling because they thought the fire got them.

But suddenly, we could hear somebody pounding at the door over and over, until . . .

BOOM!

Then Old Man Jenkins and Ned, Zed and Fred ran back to help everybody escape.

"Okay, everybody out!" Kyle yelled.

Then people started coughing and running out the door.

"How did you do that?!!!" Kyle yelled at Old Man Jenkins.

"Didn't anybody ever tell you?" Old Man Jenkins said. "Zombies are **FIREPROOF**!"

"Seriously?!!!"

"Like I said, we were born for this!"

Then they continued to help more people out of the auditorium.

Suddenly, somebody yelled . . .

"WATCH OUT!"

The roof had started falling.

Then the biggest piece of wood I had ever seen broke off the ceiling!

"BEVERLY!" the mayor lady yelled.

Just then, something came over me.

My legs moved faster than I could even think.

So, right when the mayor lady yelled, I jumped, as the fiery piece of wood came tumbling down right over Beverly . . .

Out of the Ashes

I could hear the sirens outside as the fire brigade finally got there.

They all ran inside to try to help the rest of us, who were still stuck in the auditorium.

"THE FIRE IS TOO HOT!" I heard them yelling.

But Old Man Jenkins, Ned, Zed and Fred kept running back and forth, helping pull more people out.

As for me, for some reason I couldn't move.

I could see Beverly, though. She looked like she was sleeping, but she looked okay.

Suddenly, I felt something behind me start moving.

Then I felt the big fiery piece of wood move off my back.

And next thing I know, a big, green, bony, **THREE-FINGERED HAND** reached over to me.

When I looked up, all I could see was a big green face with white hair and three big teeth smiling at me.

So Old Man Jenkins carried me, and I carried Beverly, out of the Town Hall.

And as soon as we got out of the burning building, I could hear Beverly cough and wake up.

"Beverly!" the mayor lady yelled.

I handed her over to the mayor, and she hugged Beverly with all her might.

"Thank you so much!" the mayor lady said to me. **"THANK YOU**, thank you!"

Then Kyle, Kenya, and Cassie came running over to me.

And they all gave me a big hug.

Even Cassie gave me a hug, which was a little weird.

Then a few minutes later, I felt somebody tap me on the shoulder.

"I just wanted to say thank you," Beverly said.

Then she reached over and gave me a **KISS ON THE CHEEK**.

I didn't really know what to do.

I had never been kissed before.

And I just started feeling weird all over.

So I just stood there making zombie noises.

"Urrrrggggghhh!!!"

Then everybody **BURST OUT LAUGHING**.

My New Name

Well, I was never able to show my zombie presentation at the Town Hall.

I was kind of bummed about that.

But the **GOOD NEWS** is that I'm not going to need it anymore.

Kenya told me that the town was so grateful for what the zombies did, that they decided to get rid of the No Zombie Law once and for all.

Actually, they were so grateful, they even decided to change the name of the town.

So our town is no longer going to be called HumanTown.

But they haven't found a **NEW NAME** for the town yet.

So I put in a few suggestions that I thought could work.

Like, I was thinking that ROTTINGHAM had a nice ring to it.

Or maybe FESTERTOWN.

Or I think NECROSHIRE sounds kind of nice. . .

They even decided to form a new **ZOMBIE FIRE BRIGADE**.

They put Old Man Jenkins in charge of it, and they made Ned, Zed and Fred the newest recruits.

So now, if there's ever a fire the humans can't handle, they call in the ZFB.

They're like the Zombie Fire Brigade Special Forces.

The ZFB . . . So stinkin' awesome.

As for me, I'm still just thinking about the **KISS** Beverly gave me.

I never felt that weird feeling before.

But what should I do now?

Should I, like, give her a kiss back?

But I never learned how.

Especially since zombies don't have lips . . .

Anyway, today, Kenya and Kyle said that they needed to talk to me.

It sounded kind of serious, so I started getting a **LITTLE NERVOUS**.

"Well, Zombie, I've got some good news and some bad news for you," Kenya said to me. "Which do you want to hear first?"

Oh no, not again.

I hope they don't decide to send me back to the zombie village.

That would be the worst.

"The bad news?" I said.

"Well, the bad news is that we can't be your foster family anymore," she said with tears in her eyes.

Oh, man. My worst **NIGHTMARE** had come true.

I had really grown to love Kenya and Kyle.

I mean, I can't remember ever having a mom or a dad. But they are the closest thing I ever had. And I'm going to miss them so much.

And I'm going to miss everybody else, too.

I'm going to miss Ms. Rachel and Franklin. I'm going to miss Steve. And I'm going to miss Old Man Jenkins and Ned, Zed and Fred . . .

"Well, don't you want to hear the good news?" Kenya asked.

"Sigh . . . Sure, go ahead," I said.

"Well, Kyle and I have talked about it, and Cassie too. And so, we've decided to **OFFICIALLY ADOPT** you instead."

"Wait . . . what?"

Was I hearing right?

Did she just say what I think she said?

"Are you serious?" I asked again.

"Yep. You just need to sign the paperwork, and you will officially be part of our family."

Wow! I couldn't believe this was happening.

So Kyle handed me a pen, and I wrote down my name on the dotted line: **ZOMBIE.**

But then Kenya crossed my name out.

She told me that for my adoption papers, I had to write my real name.

So I wrote down, **Z06578.**

But then Kenya crossed it out again.

This time she told me I had to write my new name.

"What do you mean?"

Then she slowly took my hand with the pen in it.

And she helped me draw all the letters:
Z . . . A . . . C . . . K.

"There. Your new name," Kenya said with tears streaming down her cheeks.

I didn't know what to say.

I have a **NEW NAME!**

And my name is Zack.

So I tried it out to see how it sounded.

"Hi, I'm Zack. But you can call me Z."

I was so happy, I just gave Kenya a big hug.

And Kenya gave me a big hug back.

And then Kyle gave us all a big hug.

And I've got to say, to this day, I'm still really impressed how they could give such big hugs . . .

. . . and hold their breath for such a **LONG TIME**.

I Guess I'm Going to Middle School

After all the excitement the past few days, Kenya decided that I had too much extra time on my hands.

So she said that she was going to enroll me in **MIDDLE SCHOOL**.

"What's middle school?" I asked her.

"It's where kids your age go to get an education," she said.

"What's an education?"

"It's when you learn things you'll need in life. Like reading, writing, history and math."

"But I can learn all that on YouTube," I said.

For some reason she just stood there, not really knowing what to say.

"Uh . . . well, let's just say it's a place where you can meet other kids your age and have **SOME FUN**," she said.

You know, that sounded great.

I really wanted to make more friends. And middle school sounded like the **PERFECT PLACE** for that.

Plus, after meeting all the nice people I've met so far, the kids in middle school are probably going to be the nicest ever.

"I'm in!" I said. "When do I start?"

"Well, the first day of school is in a few weeks. But first, we need to go shopping to get you some school supplies," Kenya said.

Whoa, I need supplies for school?

Man, this middle school thing sounds like it's going to be the best adventure yet.

So look out, Middle School, 'cause here I come!

Find Out What Happens Next In . . .

Diary of a Middle School Zombie, Book 2: Middle School Mayhem!

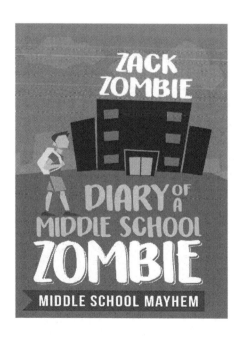

Please Leave Us a Review

Please support us by leaving a review.

The more reviews we get, the more books we will write!

And tell a friend about us right now!

They can really use the laughs, and they'll be really happy you told them about it.